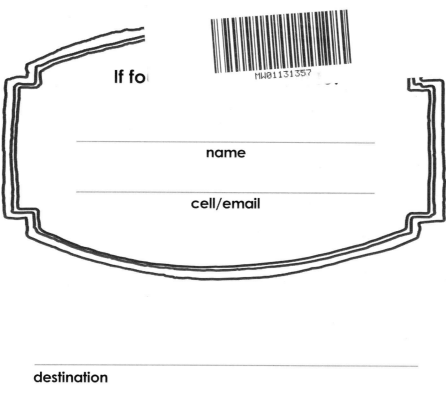

If fo

MW01131357

name

cell/email

destination

trip dates

trip companions

Indicate your starting point and then your destination(s) with arrows and/or coloring on the map below

THINGS TO REMEMBER
checklist

- ○ _____
- ○ _____
- ○ _____
- ○ _____
- ○ _____
- ○ _____
- ○ _____
- ○ _____
- ○ _____
- ○ _____
- ○ _____
- ○ _____
- ○ _____
- ○ _____
- ○ _____
- ○ _____
- ○ _____
- ○ _____
- ○ _____
- ○ _____
- ○ _____

ITINERARY

Destination: _____

Arrive: _____

Activities: _____

_____

Lodging: _____

Address: _____

_____

Notes: _____

_____

Destination: _____

Arrive: _____

Activities: _____

_____

Lodging: _____

Address: _____

_____

Notes: _____

_____

ITINERARY

Destination: _____

Arrive: _____

Activities: _____
_____

Lodging: _____

Address: _____
_____

Notes: _____
_____

Destination: _____

Arrive: _____

Activities: _____
_____

Lodging: _____

Address: _____
_____

Notes: _____
_____

ITINERARY

Destination: _____

Arrive: _____

Activities: _____

_____

Lodging: _____

Address: _____

_____

Notes: _____

_____

Destination: _____

Arrive: _____

Activities: _____

_____

Lodging: _____

Address: _____

_____

Notes: _____

_____

ITINERARY

Destination: _____

Arrive: _____

Activities: _____

_____

Lodging: _____

Address: _____

_____

Notes: _____

_____

Destination: _____

Arrive: _____

Activities: _____

_____

Lodging: _____

Address: _____

_____

Notes: _____

_____

BUDGET: _____

ACTUAL EXPENSES

DATE	DESCRIPTION	CASH, ATM, CREDIT	AMOUNT/ CURRENCY

The
LORD
YOUR
GOD
will be
WITH YOU
WHEREVER
you go

JOSHUA 1:9

JOURNAL

HIGHLIGHT OF THE DAY:

PRAYER REQUESTS:

HIGHLIGHT OF THE DAY:

_____
_____
_____
_____
_____
_____
_____
_____
_____
_____
_____
_____
_____
_____
_____

PRAYER REQUESTS:

_____
_____
_____
_____
_____
_____
_____
_____

HIGHLIGHT OF THE DAY:

PRAYER REQUESTS:

HIGHLIGHT OF THE DAY:

PRAYER REQUESTS:

HIGHLIGHT OF THE DAY:

_____
_____
_____
_____
_____
_____
_____
_____
_____
_____
_____
_____
_____
_____
_____
_____

PRAYER REQUESTS:

_____
_____
_____
_____
_____
_____
_____
_____

HIGHLIGHT OF THE DAY:

_____
_____
_____
_____
_____
_____
_____
_____
_____
_____
_____
_____
_____
_____
_____
_____

PRAYER REQUESTS:

_____
_____
_____
_____
_____
_____
_____
_____

HIGHLIGHT OF THE DAY:

_____

_____

_____

_____

_____

_____

_____

_____

_____

_____

_____

_____

_____

_____

_____

_____

PRAYER REQUESTS:

_____

_____

_____

_____

_____

_____

_____

_____

_____

HIGHLIGHT OF THE DAY:

_____

_____

_____

_____

_____

_____

_____

_____

_____

_____

_____

_____

_____

_____

PRAYER REQUESTS:

_____

_____

_____

_____

_____

_____

_____

HIGHLIGHT OF THE DAY:

PRAYER REQUESTS:

HIGHLIGHT OF THE DAY:

_____

_____

_____

_____

_____

_____

_____

_____

_____

_____

_____

_____

_____

_____

PRAYER REQUESTS:

_____

_____

_____

_____

_____

_____

_____

HIGHLIGHT OF THE DAY:

_____

_____

_____

_____

_____

_____

_____

_____

_____

_____

_____

_____

_____

_____

_____

_____

PRAYER REQUESTS:

_____

_____

_____

_____

_____

_____

_____

_____

HIGHLIGHT OF THE DAY:

_____
_____
_____
_____
_____
_____
_____
_____
_____
_____
_____
_____
_____
_____
_____
_____

PRAYER REQUESTS:

_____
_____
_____
_____
_____
_____
_____
_____

HIGHLIGHT OF THE DAY:

_____
_____
_____
_____
_____
_____
_____
_____
_____
_____
_____
_____
_____
_____

PRAYER REQUESTS:

_____
_____
_____
_____
_____
_____
_____
_____

HIGHLIGHT OF THE DAY:

_____
_____
_____
_____
_____
_____
_____
_____
_____
_____
_____
_____
_____
_____

PRAYER REQUESTS:

_____
_____
_____
_____
_____
_____
_____
_____

HIGHLIGHT OF THE DAY:

PRAYER REQUESTS:

HIGHLIGHT OF THE DAY:

_____
_____
_____
_____
_____
_____
_____
_____
_____
_____
_____
_____
_____
_____
_____
_____

PRAYER REQUESTS:

_____
_____
_____
_____
_____
_____
_____

HIGHLIGHT OF THE DAY:

PRAYER REQUESTS:

HIGHLIGHT OF THE DAY:

PRAYER REQUESTS:

HIGHLIGHT OF THE DAY:

PRAYER REQUESTS:

HIGHLIGHT OF THE DAY:

_____
_____
_____
_____
_____
_____
_____
_____
_____
_____
_____
_____
_____
_____
_____
_____

PRAYER REQUESTS:

_____
_____
_____
_____
_____
_____
_____

HIGHLIGHT OF THE DAY:

_____

_____

_____

_____

_____

_____

_____

_____

_____

_____

_____

_____

PRAYER REQUESTS:

_____

_____

_____

_____

_____

_____

_____

HIGHLIGHT OF THE DAY:

PRAYER REQUESTS:

HIGHLIGHT OF THE DAY:

PRAYER REQUESTS:

HIGHLIGHT OF THE DAY:

PRAYER REQUESTS:

HIGHLIGHT OF THE DAY:

_____
_____
_____
_____
_____
_____
_____
_____
_____
_____
_____
_____
_____
_____

PRAYER REQUESTS:

_____
_____
_____
_____
_____
_____
_____
_____

HIGHLIGHT OF THE DAY:

PRAYER REQUESTS:

HIGHLIGHT OF THE DAY:

_____
_____
_____
_____
_____
_____
_____
_____
_____
_____
_____
_____
_____
_____

PRAYER REQUESTS:

_____
_____
_____
_____
_____
_____
_____

HIGHLIGHT OF THE DAY:

_____
_____
_____
_____
_____
_____
_____
_____
_____
_____
_____
_____
_____
_____

PRAYER REQUESTS:

_____
_____
_____
_____
_____
_____
_____

HIGHLIGHT OF THE DAY:

_____

_____

_____

_____

_____

_____

_____

_____

_____

_____

_____

_____

_____

PRAYER REQUESTS:

_____

_____

_____

_____

_____

_____

_____

_____

HIGHLIGHT OF THE DAY:

PRAYER REQUESTS:

HIGHLIGHT OF THE DAY:

PRAYER REQUESTS:

HIGHLIGHT OF THE DAY:

PRAYER REQUESTS:

HIGHLIGHT OF THE DAY:

PRAYER REQUESTS:

HIGHLIGHT OF THE DAY:

PRAYER REQUESTS:

HIGHLIGHT OF THE DAY:

_____

_____

_____

_____

_____

_____

_____

_____

_____

_____

_____

_____

_____

PRAYER REQUESTS:

_____

_____

_____

_____

_____

_____

_____

HIGHLIGHT OF THE DAY:

_____

_____

_____

_____

_____

_____

_____

_____

_____

_____

_____

_____

PRAYER REQUESTS:

_____

_____

_____

_____

_____

_____

_____

HIGHLIGHT OF THE DAY:

_____

_____

_____

_____

_____

_____

_____

_____

_____

_____

_____

_____

PRAYER REQUESTS:

_____

_____

_____

_____

_____

_____

_____

HIGHLIGHT OF THE DAY:

PRAYER REQUESTS:

HIGHLIGHT OF THE DAY:

PRAYER REQUESTS:

HIGHLIGHT OF THE DAY:

PRAYER REQUESTS:

HIGHLIGHT OF THE DAY:

_____
_____
_____
_____
_____
_____
_____
_____
_____
_____
_____
_____
_____
_____
_____

PRAYER REQUESTS:

_____
_____
_____
_____
_____
_____
_____
_____

HIGHLIGHT OF THE DAY:

PRAYER REQUESTS:

HIGHLIGHT OF THE DAY:

_____
_____
_____
_____
_____
_____
_____
_____
_____
_____
_____
_____
_____
_____
_____

PRAYER REQUESTS:

_____
_____
_____
_____
_____
_____
_____
_____

HIGHLIGHT OF THE DAY:

_____
_____
_____
_____
_____
_____
_____
_____
_____
_____
_____
_____
_____
_____
_____
_____

PRAYER REQUESTS:

_____
_____
_____
_____
_____
_____
_____

HIGHLIGHT OF THE DAY:

_____
_____
_____
_____
_____
_____
_____
_____
_____
_____
_____
_____
_____

PRAYER REQUESTS:

_____
_____
_____
_____
_____
_____
_____

... AND WHAT DOTH THE *Lord* REQUIRE OF THEE,

BUT TO DO

JUSTLY

AND TO LOVE

MERCY

AND TO WALK

HUMBLY

with thy God.

MICAH 6:8

POST TRIP

THANK YOU NOTE REMINDERS

Thank those who helped to make your trip possible

BEST MEMORY

_____

_____

_____

_____

_____

_____

_____

_____

_____

WORST MEMORY

_____

_____

_____

_____

_____

_____

_____

_____

_____

What did God teach me while I was on this trip?

_____

_____

_____

_____

_____

_____

_____

_____

What did I learn about myself?

_____

_____

_____

_____

_____

_____

_____

_____

_____

_____

OTHER NOTES

AUTOGRAPHS

Made in United States
North Haven, CT
17 July 2023

39162480R00085